zendoodle

M000038961

Creative Sensations

Other great books in the series

zendoodle coloring

zendoodle pocket coloring

Calming Swirls
Enchanting Gardens

zendoodle coloring

Calming Swirls
Creative Sensations
Enchanting Gardens
Inspiring Zendalas

Keep Calm and Color On
Keep Happy and Color On
Keep Merry and Color On

Creative Sensations

Hypnotic Patterns to Color and Display

illustrations by

Julia Snegireva

ST. MARTIN'S GRIFFIN
NEW YORK

ZENDOODLE POCKET COLORING: CREATIVE SENSATIONS.
Copyright © 2016 by St. Martin's Press. All rights reserved.
Printed in the United States of America. For information, address
St. Martin's Press, 175 Fifth Avenue, New York, N.Y. 10010.

www.stmartins.com

ISBN 978-1-250-10512-7 (trade paperback)

St. Martin's Griffin books may be purchased for educational, business, or promotional
use. For information on bulk purchases, please contact the Macmillan Corporate and
Premium Sales Department at 1-800-221-7945, extension 5442, or write to
specialmarkets@macmillan.com.

First Edition: January 2016

10 9 8 7 6 5 4 3 2 1